SAN JOSE SHARKS

BY LUKE HANLON

Book design by Maggie Villaume
Cover design by Maggie Villaume

Photographs ©: Tony Avelar/AP Images, cover; John Locher/AP Images,
4–5, 23; Josie Lepe/AP Images, 7; Chris Brown/CSM/ZUMA Wire/AP
Images, 9; John G. Mabanglo/AP Images, 10–11; John Discher/AP Images,
12; AP Images, 14; Holly Stein/AP Images, 16–17; Paul Sakuma/AP Images,
19; Kyle Ericson/AP Images, 20; Chris Carlson/AP Images, 24–25; Marcio
Jose Sanchez/AP Images, 27; Jeff Chiu/AP Images, 28

Press Box Books, an imprint of Press Room Editions.

ISBN
978-1-63494-680-3 (library bound)
978-1-63494-704-6 (paperback)
978-1-63494-750-3 (epub)
978-1-63494-728-2 (hosted ebook)

Library of Congress Control Number: 2022919287

Distributed by North Star Editions, Inc.
2297 Waters Drive
Mendota Heights, MN 55120
www.northstareditions.com

Printed in the United States of America
082023

ABOUT THE AUTHOR
Luke Hanlon is a sportswriter and editor based in Minneapolis.

TABLE OF CONTENTS

1

The San Jose Sharks scored the second-most goals in the NHL during the 2018–19 regular season, with 289.

SHARK
BITE

The San Jose Sharks quickly fell behind 3–1 in the opening series of the 2019 National Hockey League (NHL) postseason. The Vegas Golden Knights needed just one more win to move on. That's when the Sharks found their bite.

San Jose won the next two games to force a Game 7. This time, the Golden Knights were ready. William Karlsson put them up

1–0 in the first period. By early in the third, they led 3–0. But with around 11 minutes left, the game was shaken up.

Vegas center Cody Eakin was given a penalty for cross-checking Joe Pavelski. The hit knocked the Sharks captain out of the game. The Sharks were given a five-minute power play.

San Jose scored a goal just seconds after play restarted. Winger Kevin Labanc found teammate Logan Couture wide open. The goal gave the SAP Center some life. The Sharks struck again less than a minute later.

The puck reached defenseman Erik Karlsson, who sent a rocket at goal. Teammate Tomas Hertl stuck out his stick.

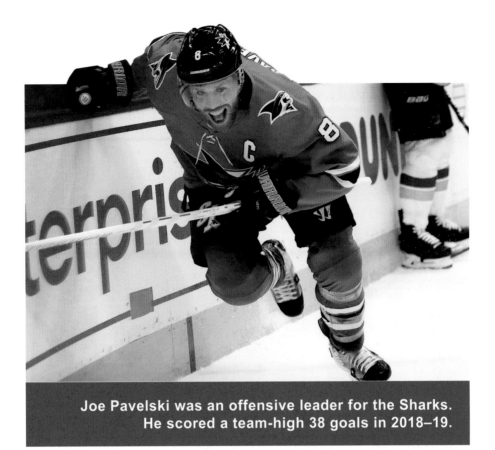

Joe Pavelski was an offensive leader for the Sharks. He scored a team-high 38 goals in 2018–19.

His touch was enough to send it past Vegas goalie Marc-Andre Fleury.

San Jose found its equalizer soon after. Couture poked the puck in right in front of the Vegas goal. The Sharks' fans lost it. The game was all tied up. And the Sharks soon took the lead on another power play. It was a low shot from Labanc that sneaked past Fleury. The five-minute power play had yielded four goals.

But the game wasn't quite over. The Golden Knights managed to get a goal in the final minute of the third period. A strike by Vegas center Jonathan Marchessault tied the game at 4–4. The game would have to be decided in overtime.

It took until the last two minutes of the period for someone to score. Erik Karlsson laid the puck off perfectly for Barclay Goodrow. The winger was

•SUPERSTAR PERFORMANCE

The Sharks' 2019 playoff run ended in the conference finals. But Logan Couture still showed his star qualities. He scored 14 goals in 20 playoff games. That was the highest goal tally in the 2019 playoffs.

Barclay Goodrow celebrates after scoring the series-winning goal against the Vegas Golden Knights in 2019.

suddenly one-on-one with Fleury. Goodrow was too quick for the goalie. He tucked the winning goal away. The SAP Center burst into celebration. And the Sharks advanced to the next round of the playoffs.

2

George Gund celebrates the unveiling of the Sharks colors and logo for the first time in 1991.

BLOOD IN THE
WATER

The Minnesota North Stars tried to move to San Jose, California, during the 1980s. Owners George and Gordon Gund agreed to a deal in 1990. But the NHL didn't want the team to move. Instead, the NHL allowed the Gunds to sell the North Stars to another owner. In return, they were allowed to start a new team in San Jose with half of the North Stars roster.

Sergei Makarov (right) and Sandis Ozolinsh (left) helped improve the Sharks with a combined 132 points in 1993–94.

The Sharks began playing in the 1991–92 season. It didn't go well. San Jose had the fewest points in the league. Things didn't get better in their second season either. The Sharks suffered a

17-game losing streak. They ended the season with an NHL-record 71 losses.

Fans still flocked to the team. The Sharks sold $150 million worth of merchandise in 1992–93. That was by far the most in the league. The extra money helped the Sharks build a new arena. The team started playing in the San Jose Arena for the 1993–94 season. It became known as the "Shark Tank." The Shark

OWNERS' CHOICE

A fan vote was held to decide the name for the new team in San Jose. "Blades" ended up winning. The owners didn't want the name to be tied to weapons, however. They went with the runner-up name, which was the Sharks. There is a large shark population in the Pacific Ocean off the coast of California.

The Sharks celebrate their Game 7 victory over the Detroit Red Wings in the 1994 Western Conference playoffs.

Tank hosted one of the loudest fan groups in the NHL.

The Sharks turned things around quickly and made the playoffs in 1994. Sergei Makarov was a huge reason. It was his first season in San Jose. But he propelled the Sharks' attack with a team-high 68 points in 1993–94. They even beat the heavily favored Detroit Red Wings in the first round of the playoffs. The Sharks fell to the Toronto Maple Leafs in the second round. But it was a proud time for San Jose. The Sharks had taken two strong teams to seven games.

The Sharks were right back in the playoffs in 1995. They met the Calgary Flames in the first round. The high-scoring series went to seven games. The teams headed to overtime in Game 7 tied 4–4. Sharks winger Ray Whitney finally ended the game in double overtime. His deflected goal was exactly what the Sharks needed. But the Red Wings got revenge in the next round. They swept the Sharks out of the playoffs.

3

The 1996–97 San Jose Sharks were last in the NHL with 211 goals in the regular season.

SHARK
ATTACK

San Jose couldn't continue its playoff streak for long. The Sharks became one of the worst teams in the league for the next two seasons. But that poor record came with a reward. The Sharks got the second pick in the 1997 NHL Draft. They selected Patrick Marleau.

The center was ready to play in 1997–98 as an 18-year-old. Marleau was part of a new wave of young players taking the ice in San Jose. Players like Jeff Friesen and Andrei Zyuzin had promise. The team made another big addition before the season. San Jose hired Darryl Sutter as its head coach.

The Sharks improved for five straight years under Sutter. He led San Jose to its first winning record in 1999–2000. The team played even better in 2001–02. San Jose finished with 99 points. That was enough to win the Pacific Division for the first time. The Sharks took down the Phoenix Coyotes in the first round of the playoffs. Marleau tallied six points in five games to lead the Sharks. But the team then fell in seven games to the Colorado Avalanche in the next round.

Patrick Marleau (right) got off to a fast start in the NHL. He scored 45 points as a 19-year-old in 1998–99.

Sutter couldn't reach those heights again. He was fired during the 2002–03 season. But the Sharks bounced back quickly. Marleau and young winger Jonathan Cheechoo provided the scoring. Meanwhile, Evgeni Nabokov was one of the league's best goaltenders.

Evgeni Nabokov (left) makes a save against the St. Louis Blues in the first round of the 2004 Stanley Cup playoffs.

They led the Sharks to another division title in 2003–04. They easily beat the St. Louis Blues in the first round. San Jose then took down the Avalanche in six games. That secured the team's first trip to the conference finals. But the following series was tough. The Calgary Flames shut down Marleau and Cheechoo. The Sharks lost in six games.

San Jose made a big trade during the 2005–06 season. They traded with the Boston Bruins for center Joe Thornton. He was one of the league's best players. The Sharks thought he was the missing piece of a title-contending team. Marleau and Thornton kept the Sharks competitive for years.

AWARDS GALORE

Joe Thornton won the Art Ross Trophy in 2005–06. That is given to the player with the most points each season. He also won the Hart Memorial Trophy, which is given to the league's most valuable player. Jonathan Cheechoo led the league with 56 goals that season. That earned him the Maurice "Rocket" Richard Trophy.

PATRICK MARLEAU

Patrick Marleau's rookie season on the Sharks came when he was 18. When he played his last game for San Jose, he was 41. Not every year was with the Sharks. But San Jose was where the center etched his name in NHL history.

Marleau quickly became San Jose's biggest star. He was a reliable goal scorer for years. He racked up 522 for the Sharks. He tallied 1,111 points as well. Both were the most in team history when Marleau retired.

Durability was Marleau's best skill. He missed only 31 games in his entire career. And he played a team-record 1,607 games over 21 seasons with the Sharks.

Marleau's final NHL season was 2020–21. He skated in his 1,768th NHL game that year. That passed Gordie Howe for the most games played in league history. Breaking a record held by "Mr. Hockey" proved Marleau's passion for the game.

Patrick Marleau receives an ovation
in 2021 for passing Gordie Howe for

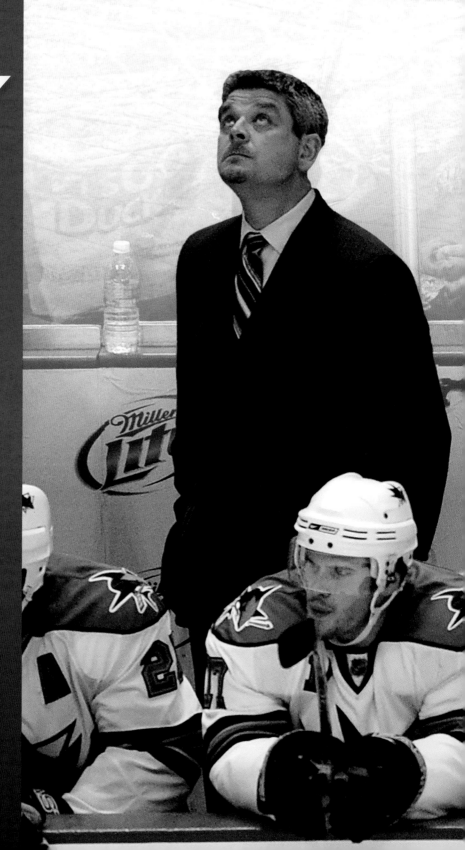

4

Todd McLellan watches as the Sharks battle the Anaheim Ducks in the first round of the 2009 Stanley Cup playoffs.

OUT AT SEA

Trading for Joe Thornton helped turn the Sharks into one of the best teams in the Western Conference. He led San Jose to four straight division titles from 2008 to 2011. Head coach Todd McLellan was also huge for the Sharks. His first season was 2008–09. San Jose improved quickly under McLellan. The Sharks made runs to the conference finals in 2010 and 2011. But they fell short both times.

The Sharks' postseason performances hit a new low soon after. They faced the Los Angeles Kings in the first round of the 2014 playoffs. San Jose went up 3–0 in the series. The team was looking at a sweep. But the Kings won the next four games to stun San Jose. The Sharks continued to collapse after that. They missed the playoffs in 2014–15.

It was their first time without playoff hockey in 11 seasons. That marked the end of McLellan's run. He left as the winningest coach in team history. New coach Peter DeBoer brought new life to the Sharks franchise.

The Sharks' play didn't drop under Peter DeBoer. They made the playoffs in each of the four full seasons that he was the coach.

The Sharks still had a talented roster built around Joe Thornton and Patrick Marleau. Joe Pavelski and Logan Couture were still scoring goals. And defenseman Brent Burns added more goals from the blue line. The Sharks made it to the 2015–16 conference finals with this core.

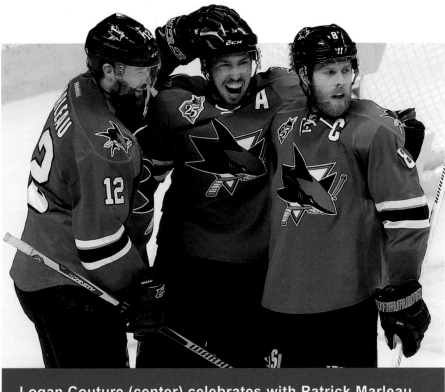
Logan Couture (center) celebrates with Patrick Marleau (left) and Joe Pavelski (right) after scoring in Game 6 against the St. Louis Blues.

The Sharks took a 3–2 series lead against the St. Louis Blues into Game 6. Pavelski opened the scoring early. The other four members of San Jose's core all picked up assists in the game. A late empty-net goal from Couture secured a 5–2 win. That sent the Sharks to their first Stanley Cup Final. However, the Pittsburgh Penguins proved to be too much to handle. The Sharks lost in six games.

The Sharks made the playoffs for three more years, including the run to the conference finals against Vegas in 2019. Gradually, their stars left or retired. It was the first major reset for the Sharks in around two decades. Despite never having seen their team lift the Stanley Cup, Sharks fans had high hopes for the future.

SHARK MANIA

The Sharks have two traditions that celebrate their name. Before every home game, the team skates out of a 17-foot (5.2 m) inflatable shark's mouth. The arena also plays the theme music from the movie *Jaws* before every San Jose power play.

● SAN JOSE SHARKS
QUICK STATS

TEAM HISTORY: San Jose Sharks (1991–)

STANLEY CUP CHAMPIONSHIPS: 0

KEY COACHES:

- Ron Wilson (2002–08): 206 wins, 122 losses, 19 ties, 38 overtime losses

- Todd McLellan (2008–15): 311 wins, 163 losses, 66 overtime losses

- Peter DeBoer (2015–19): 198 wins, 129 losses, 34 overtime losses

HOME ARENA: SAP Center (San Jose, CA)

MOST CAREER POINTS: Patrick Marleau (1,111)

MOST CAREER GOALS: Patrick Marleau (522)

MOST CAREER ASSISTS: Joe Thornton (804)

MOST CAREER SHUTOUTS: Evgeni Nabokov (50)

Stats are accurate through the 2021–22 season.

GLOSSARY

ASSIST
A pass, rebound, or deflection that results in a goal.

BLUE LINE
One of two lines on a hockey rink that divides the rink into a defensive zone, a neutral zone, and an offensive zone.

CAPTAIN
A team's leader.

CONFERENCE
A smaller group of teams that make up a part of a sports league.

DRAFT
An event that allows teams to choose new players coming into the league.

MERCHANDISE
Goods to be bought and sold.

ROOKIE
A first-year player.

SWEEP
When a team wins all the games in a series.

TO LEARN
MORE

BOOKS

Davidson, B. Keith. *NHL*. New York: Crabtree Publishing, 2022.

Doeden, Matt. *G.O.A.T. Hockey Teams*. Minneapolis: Lerner Publications, 2021.

Duling, Kaitlyn. *Women in Hockey*. Lake Elmo, MN: Focus Readers, 2020.

MORE INFORMATION

To learn more about the San Jose Sharks, go to **pressboxbooks.com/AllAccess**.

These links are routinely monitored and updated to provide the most current information available.

INDEX